# Portland,
*in Your*

Your Guide to an Hour, a Day, or a Weekend in the City

**INSIDERS'** GUIDE®

GUILFORD, CONNECTICUT
AN IMPRINT OF GLOBE PEQUOT PRESS

# Contents

# Welcome to Portland

Compared with cities such as Los Angeles, San Francisco, or even Seattle, Portland is small. But we like it that way. Though Portland contributes its share to cyberspace, it is also concerned with human space. Portland is the home of groundbreaking biomedical research and world-class firms for animation, advertising, and athletic wear. Yet it is also renowned for its amiable, everyday civility, for its dedication to wise planning and public transportation, for its charming neighborhoods, for its bookstores, sidewalk cafes, and pubs. The parks contain more forest than any city in the nation. People ride their bikes or walk to work. The library serves coffee. Portland is a city where the fire department will still come to your block party.

Portland is an attractive city with a friendly skyline in a beautiful region of the country. Its setting, in a fertile valley ringed by mountains and bordered by the Columbia and Willamette Rivers, shapes the character of the city in ways that residents tend to take for granted. But the beautiful country surrounding us and within the city itself commands great loyalty—a loyalty that extends to the way we live and work. Many local businesses, for example, are consciously devoted to growing and creating products that draw from our regional abundance, and many others are devoted to using and promoting these products. We work hard to maintain our quality of life.

We are also a playful city. Citizens prize their parks and libraries. Neighborhood coffee shops and brewpubs are busy long into the night. Workers may leave the downtown area at 5:00 p.m., but they are soon replaced by recreators attending the theater, the movies, the ballet, the symphony, or the opera, strolling the boulevards, stopping for dinner or a glass of wine. On the weekends, crowds gather at the Saturday Market, at the Farmers' Market, at the river. Or people

**i** Area Codes and 10-Digit Dialing: Due to a proliferation of telephone numbers, Portland, like most metropolitan areas, has added area codes in recent years. The area codes that serve Portland are (503) and (971). When you make a call in the Portland area, you will need to dial the area code first, then the number—all 10 digits. It won't be a long-distance call unless you dial a "1" first, which would make 11 digits.

head up to the mountains or to the coast. We know how to have a good time.

This appealing mixture of nature and culture, of sophistication and friendliness, draws people from all over the world, and sometimes when they have visited, they want to stay. Who can blame them?

# Overview

The Portland Metropolitan area comprises Multnomah, Washington, and Clackamas Counties, as well as the southern edge of Clark County in Washington State across the Columbia River to the north. The area is home to nearly two million people who live, work, and play in one of the most beautiful urban areas in the country—at least, that's what we think.

Portland sits just to the south of the confluence of the Willamette and Columbia Rivers; it is indeed a port city. It is situated approximately 70 miles from the Pacific Ocean and connects to the Pacific via the Columbia River. Its busy shipping schedule makes it the third-leading commercial maritime center on the West Coast. A significant portion of its freight is eastern Oregon grain, barged down the Columbia, loaded into huge grain elevators, and poured into freighters heading for Asia. On the receiving end, Portland is the third-largest West Coast port for ships bringing Japanese cars into the United States.

Portland is known as the "City of Roses," and it possesses the ideal climate in which to grow these lovely flowers. Each June, they are celebrated with

a party called the Rose Festival, an event that includes three parades, a carnival, the crowning of a queen, and a visit from a dozen ships from the U.S. Navy, U.S. Coast Guard, and the Canadian Navy and Coast Guard.

Part of what makes those roses grow, of course, is rain. While Portland has 82 days per year when the sky is blue and the sun is shining, it also has, on the average, 82 partly cloudy days and 220 cloudy days per year, with 165 of those coming with at least some precipitation.

Another element that defines the essence of Portland is the 40-mile Willamette River Greenway, a network of pedestrian and bike trails on both sides of the Willamette that will eventually stretch into a 140-mile-long system connecting 30 parks. Currently it is a paved trail that can take you from Oaks Park in Southeast Portland north along the Willamette to the Steel Bridge. From there you can cross the river to Northwest Portland and follow it south through Tom McCall Park to Willamette Park off Macadam Avenue.

Walking in Portland is one of its chief pleasures. Miles of paths line the waterfront, inviting pedestrians to ramble. Not only is the downtown area clean and well maintained, but the little villagelike neighborhoods that make up the city encourage residents to walk to the store, the bank, the library, dinner, even work. The city has found that promoting foot traffic is a smart business move. And moving your legs to get to your business can also be a smart move; on any given morning, you will find pedestrians strolling across downtown bridges, taking advantage of their commute time to exercise their legs, minds, and souls as they prepare for their day. If you're thinking of relocating, you might consider the walking potential of any prospective neighborhoods. You might even find a great job in your own neighborhood and be able to walk to work.

# Planning Your Itinerary

Whether travelers come as part of a group or independently, they find a full array of activities in Portland—all of which are explored throughout this guide. We will let you plan your own itinerary, but first you need to understand the lay of the land.

Portland is divided into eastern and western halves by the Willamette River. It is further divided by Burnside Street, which runs east and west, into four quadrants: Southwest, Northwest, Southeast, and Northeast. A fifth "quadrant," North Portland, the portion west of Williams Avenue, extends from the Broadway Bridge to the Columbia River; however, for the purposes of this book, listings in North Portland and

**i** Portland has a number of colorful nicknames: the City of Roses, Puddletown, and Bridgetown, as well as PDX, our airport code. And we are still known as Stumptown, from the hundreds of fir stumps left in the streets by hasty 19th-century builders. Hinting at our future commitment to good public transportation, early city officials painted them white to warn wagoneers out after dark.

Northeast Portland have been kept together.

Few things define Portland as much as its neighborhoods, however, and so to these we now turn.

### Southwest Portland

Southwest Portland encompasses the downtown area, stretching west beyond Washington Park and south along the Willamette River. The result is an urban village cradled by a friendly wilderness. The downtown area is composed of short blocks, platted in the 19th century to contain lots of little stores and cross streets, thus limiting the size and height of new construction.

**i** Portland's Washington Park MAX station is the home of the deepest light-rail stop in the nation, at 260 feet below Earth's surface. En route to the elevators that take you to the zoo, stop to look at the core rock samples and read about the geology of the West Hills.

A good place to start a tour of the Southwest is Pioneer Courthouse Square (www.pioneercourthousesquare.org), which is bordered by Yamhill Street, Morrison Street, 6th Avenue, and Broadway. This is the piazza that anchors the city, full of tourists, office workers eating lunch, families with children, and all the characters that city plazas attract. It is also noted for its waterfall fountain, its imaginative sculpture, and an echo chamber—if you face the steps of the small amphitheater while standing on the round marble stone, you can create a cascade of sound by just saying hello.

### Northwest Portland

Northwest Portland is characterized by its creative energy, both in its industrially chic Pearl District and in its beautiful Victorian district, Nob Hill. Northwest Portland is also the home of Old Town on the north side of Burnside Street and Chinatown and the Skidmore District. Chinatown, with its entrance at 4th Avenue and Burnside Street, is an Asian-American neighborhood with grocery stores, restaurants, and art galleries.

The Portland Classical Chinese Garden, a standout in the district, is one of the few authentic classical-style Chinese gardens in the United States.

### Southeast Portland

Southeast Portland is a sprawling district characterized by parks, funky residential neighborhoods, alternative-lifestyle shops, Reed College, a riverfront industrial area, and an emerging indie business scene. Lower Burnside is the epicenter of new urban energy and its attendant development.

### North/Northeast Portland

Northeast Portland and its neighbor North Portland are home to the same blend of industry, commerce, culture, and houses that characterize the rest of the city. Beautiful older houses line tree-shaded streets in neighborhoods such as Laurelhurst, Irvington, and Alameda. Attractive shopping areas draw people from around the region. The popular Lloyd Center is the largest single shopping destination in the area (see Shopping). By light rail, Lloyd Center is just minutes from downtown.

# Getting Here, Getting Around

Bordered by mountains, flanked by rivers, surrounded by fertile farmland, the Portland Metro area is well known for its beautiful setting. But don't let those high mountains fool you: Portland accommodates many modes of transportation and allows easy travel once you arrive. The territory is well served by trains, planes, and buses, and its public transportation system is comprehensive.

Portland International Airport, or PDX, is the regional airport for all of Oregon and much of southwestern Washington. From here, in addition to its national and international service, commercial air service provides flights to Eugene, Salem, and Medford. Feeder and regional airlines also serve Pendleton and Klamath Falls in eastern and southern Oregon, in addition to providing flights to Newport and North Bend on the Oregon coast. Flights to the airport in Redmond, Oregon, will take you to the popular resorts and natural attractions of Bend and the rest of central Oregon.

Portland's Amtrak station operates trains to and from Seattle, Los Angeles, and Chicago, as well as nearby towns such as Corvallis and Eugene. Greyhound

buses provide ground transportation in all directions, and buses run regularly to and from Seattle, Tacoma, and Olympia; Boise; Denver; Salt Lake City; and major cities in California.

Two interstate highways intersect Portland. Interstate 84 runs east and west through the Columbia Gorge from Portland to Idaho and beyond, and Interstate 5 runs through Portland on its way from Canada to Mexico. Often you'll hear references to the I-5 Corridor, the stretch of I-5 that runs from Portland to Eugene.

From I-5, routes travel west across the Coastal Range to the Pacific Ocean and U.S. Highway 101 and east through several mountain passes, across the Cascade Mountains to central and eastern Oregon. During the winter, some of the passes through the Cascades are closed. Those that remain open year-round may be subject to periodic closures due to weather. Traction devices (chains and studded tires) are often required for winter travel through the Cascades (and at times, through the Coastal Range). The Oregon State Police strictly enforce laws requiring motorists to carry traction devices.

You will find that Portland is not difficult to navigate once you understand its idiosyncrasies. As we described in Planning Your Itinerary, the city is divided into east and west by the Willamette River and north and south by Burnside

Street. These serve as your orientation marks, and addresses and street numbers are organized around them. If you're on Southwest 5th Avenue downtown, you'll know that you're 5 blocks west of the Willamette River. Similarly, Burnside Street is the starting point for street addresses, and these rise in number the farther north or south that you travel from Burnside. So if your Southwest 5th Avenue address happens to be 423, you'll know that you're about 4 blocks south of Burnside.

## *Getting Here*

### By Air

**Portland International Airport**
7000 Northeast Airport Way
503-460-4234, 877-739-4636
www.flypdx.com)

Portland International Airport—which we call PDX (its aeronautical code)—is notably clean, light, and pleasant, with many comforts to serve the weary traveler. At times it feels more like an upscale shopping mall than an airport, and indeed, it has won top honors for its shopping and concessions from airport retailers across the nation—as well as accolades from the travelers who actually use them. At certain times of the year, particularly in the fall, early morning fog can wreak havoc with departure times at PDX, and some regional flights are affected by local weather at their intended destinations.

Once you've arrived at PDX, you'll find a cadre of helpers to provide directions; they can point you to your connecting flight gate, the correct baggage carousel, or any other location within the airport complex. Airport service workers offer transportation to and from the passenger gates in electric carts. They can also point out the specially designated "meet and greet" areas: Unticketed persons are forbidden to go past security checkpoints, so if someone is meeting you, you will find them there.

## Ground Transportation and Rental Cars

Transportation from the airport is available by light rail, taxi, and other ride services. You can, of course, also rent cars. Car rental agencies are on the terminal grounds, though several of them have only kiosks there.

## Light Rail: The Red Line

Portland's light-rail system, MAX, is a convenient way to get downtown from the airport. The Red Line serves downtown and PDX: It takes about 40 minutes and costs $2.05, one-way. Trains are just outside the baggage claim area, and they are well marked with prominent signs. To take the Red Line into town, purchase your ticket prior to boarding the train at one of the vending machines inside the terminal, near the doors leading to the trains, or outside near the track. You'll need to buy an all-zone ticket.

The vending machines will accept $1 bills, change, and—for several tickets—credit cards. (You can buy tickets ahead of time online, if you are well organized; see http://trimet.org/store/index.htm.) Once you've bought your ticket, be sure to validate it in the machine prior to boarding, and hang onto this ticket for your entire ride—it acts as proof of payment. Cheerful TriMet transit authority employees are usually standing by to help you figure out tickets, destinations, and other problems. Trains to downtown leave about every 15 minutes at peak times and slightly less often at other times. See the TriMet entry later in this chapter for more information on the MAX line.

## Taxis and Shuttles

Taxi service from the airport is permitted only by those companies licensed by the city of Portland. These companies are **Broadway Cab** (503) 227-1234, **Green Cab** (503) 234-1414, **New Rose City Cab** (503) 282-7707, **Portland Taxi** (503) 256-5400, and **Radio Cab** (503) 227-1212. Taxis to downtown Portland should cost $25 to $30; the trip downtown takes from 20 to 40 minutes. In addition, a number of hotels provide their own free shuttle services: Double-Tree Hotels offer shuttles every 30 minutes, and the Holiday Inn, every hour. Other hotels may also offer this service, and you can find out which ones by checking the Reservation Board in the baggage claim area. Some of these courtesy shuttles run regularly at scheduled times, while others must be summoned.

You will also find a number of other shuttle and towncar services in the Ground Transportation Center. The prices for these will vary depending on the number of passengers, the distance you will travel, and the luxuriousness of the vehicle. Starting airport rates typically run from $15 to $35. Companies known to be reliable include **Blue Star** (503) 249-1837, **Eagle Towncar** (503) 222-2763, **Pacific Executive** (503) 234-2400, **Willamette Express Shuttle** (503) 280-9883, and **Green Shuttle** (503) 234-1414.

## Rental Cars

For car rentals at the airport, go to the parking garage's first floor. The agencies with offices in the garage include **Avis Rent-A-Car** (503) 249-4950, **Budget Rent-A-Car** (503) 249-4556, **Dollar Rent-A-Car** (503) 249-4793, **Hertz Rent-A-Car** (503) 249-8216, and **Enterprise** (503) 252-1500. Some car rental agencies have kiosks just outside the car rental center in the parking garage; these include **Alamo/National** (503) 249-4900. For more information see the section on renting a car, later in this chapter.

Once you've left the airport, it should take 20 to 30 minutes to reach downtown, and there are clear directions to the freeways from the airport

access roads. Airport traffic is funneled onto Interstate 205. To reach downtown, you will take I-205 South to the I-84 West exit. Follow I-84 to I-5, where you should follow the signs to City Center.

## By Train

**Amtrak at Union Station**
800 Northwest 6th Ave.
(503) 273-4865 (station information)
(503) 273-4866 (daily arrival and departure information)
(800) 872-7245 (reservations and schedule information)
www.amtrakcascades.com

One of Portland's most charming postcard views is Union Station, with its brick clock tower that actually keeps good time. Portland's Union Station is an important stop on several major rail routes. The Empire Builder, a passenger train that originates in Chicago, stops here, as does another classic train, the Coast Starlight, which runs daily from Los Angeles to Seattle. Amtrak's Cascade route features the state-of-the-art, Spanish-built, high-speed Talgo, an ultramodern "tilt" train that runs from Eugene to Vancouver, British Columbia. If you're a train fan, consider a day trip north to Seattle or Olympia on the Talgo. If you tire of the scenery, you can plug in your laptop and settle in with one of the microbrews served on board.

## By Interstate Bus

### Greyhound Lines
550 Northwest 6th Ave.
(503) 243-2361, (800) 231-2222
www.greyhound.com

Portland's Greyhound Lines bus station is a remarkably clean and modern terminal on the far northern end of the city's transit mall adjacent to Amtrak's Union Station, both of which are a short walk from downtown. The Greyhound terminal is included in the public transportation system's Fareless Square, so once you've arrived, it is easy to connect with city buses.

## By Car

As the Portland Metro region has grown, so has the amount of traffic and congestion. During rush hours, 7:00 to 9:00 a.m. and again from 3:30 to 6:00 p.m., car and bus traffic pours into downtown from all directions. Those going to high-tech jobs in Washington County have a reverse commute, but their numbers create rush-hour traffic in both directions on freeways, the region's main arterials, downtown streets, and often on secondary streets.

You will want to bear in mind a few things as you travel the city. The downtown area is laid on a grid of one-way streets, so look carefully before making a turn lest you find yourself heading straight into traffic. The major southbound street is Broadway; the major northbound street is 4th Avenue; 10th and 11th Avenues are also important north- and southbound streets. Naito Parkway (formerly called Front Avenue) runs along the Willamette River; it permits both north- and southbound traffic. Important eastbound streets are Market, Alder, and Columbia; westbound arterials include Clay, Washington, and Jefferson. Burnside allows both east- and westbound traffic, but the places where you are allowed to make a left turn off Burnside are rare in the downtown area.

Two major streets, 6th Avenue and 5th Avenue, are the arterials for the bus system downtown, making up a large

**i** Oregon is one of two states in the country that prohibit self-serve gas stations. Don't try to fill your tank yourself, or you will be descended upon by irate attendants. Unfortunately, our laws do not mandate oil checks or cleaning of windshields; these you may have to do yourself.

component of the transit mall. These streets have also been transformed into light-rail conduits. This is helpful to know if you are planning to ride the bus or train, but you also need to know it if you're driving downtown because you must be alert to the traffic markings. Some blocks along these streets are for mass transit only, some blocks allow cars, and some blocks funnel cars right into "turn only" lanes. Car drivers should also pay attention to the signs that warn you not to turn on red lights, because these signs prevent cars from being hit by MAX trains. Furthermore, you must allow buses the right-of-way if you are driving behind them and they are signaling to pull into traffic. A flashing red yield sign on the bus will let you know if you are hogging the road illegally.

You should know a few other important streets and highways in the area. I–205, the freeway that takes you to the airport, will also take you south around the eastern edge of the city of Portland to communities such as Oregon City and West Linn before it reconnects with I–5

just south of Lake Oswego. To the north, I–205 takes you across the Columbia River into Washington State, hooking up with I–5 north of Vancouver. State Highways 99E and 99W are also critical roads. They are the eastern and western sides of Highway 99, the principal thoroughfare of Oregon before I–5 was built, which splits in two just north of Eugene. The directions "W" and "E" designate which side of the Willamette River you are on. South of Portland, Highway 99W is also called the West Pacific Highway, but in the city limits it has several names. In order, from south to north, they are Barbur Boulevard, Naito Parkway, and, when it finally crosses the Willamette again, North Interstate Avenue.

Similarly, the East Pacific Highway, 99E, is also called McLoughlin Boulevard from Oregon City until just north of the Ross Island Bridge. At that point, Highway 99E splits into a northbound arterial called Grand Avenue and a southbound arterial called Martin Luther King Jr. Boulevard (or MLK). These two rejoin north of Broadway to form Martin Luther King Jr. Boulevard. Both Highways 99W and 99E merge into I–5 immediately south of the Columbia River.

Broadway can also be confusing because it extends from Northeast Portland (where it is called "Northeast Broadway") across the Broadway Bridge to downtown Portland, where it is technically named "Southwest Broadway." But nobody calls it that—downtowners call it just plain "Broadway." While Broadway passes through downtown, it takes the place of 7th Avenue, so you will find it between 6th and 8th Avenues. And after it passes through downtown, it turns into Broadway Drive. Look carefully at the street address of your destination.

Cars, buses, streetcars, light rail, bikes, pedestrians, and the occasional horse all share the streets of Portland. The freeways have additional factors to consider. Traffic not only consists of cars, motorcycles, vans, and the ubiquitous sport-utility vehicles, but also heavy trucks. It is not uncommon to find triple-trailers (legal on some Oregon freeways) and muddy, heavily loaded log trucks bumper to bumper with everyone else.

## Getting Around
### Parking

Parking on downtown streets during business hours takes some patience, especially given downtown Portland's grid of one-way streets. Meters generally cost $1.25 per hour and allow parking for periods of time between 15 minutes and 5 hours. Don't try to stay past the time allotted: Cars are frequently monitored to make sure drivers don't overstay their welcome. Once a parking patrol member has started to write you a citation, it is yours. Portland has replaced its old coin-operated parking meters with

SmartMeter stations. These central pay station machines work by issuing paper stubs that you adhere to your curbside window.

Municipal and private parking garages are an alternative to on-street meters. There are six clearly marked Smart Park garages in downtown Portland, where parking is $1.25 an hour for the first four hours (after that, it's $3 per hour). On the weekend you can park at Smart Park for $2 for the whole evening when entering after 6:00 p.m. or all day on weekends for only $5. Many downtown merchants will validate your Smart Park ticket for two hours of free parking if you spend $25 or more in their stores. Private garages and parking lots charge anywhere from $2 to more than $10 an hour, depending on the time of day you arrive.

Outside of downtown Portland and popular shopping and eating districts such as Northwest 23rd Avenue and Northeast Broadway, parking is easier. At the large malls and shopping centers and popular attractions, such as the Oregon Zoo, you can expect the usual automobile anarchy.

## Public Transportation
### TriMet
4012 Southeast 17th Ave.
(503) 238-RIDE (trip information)
www.trimet.org

TriMet is Portland's award-winning mass transit system. TriMet comprises the bus, light-rail, and streetcar systems, and it is noted for its efficiency, comprehensiveness, and accommodation—for example, it uses modernized low-level vehicles for easy boarding and unloading. MAX reaches from eastern Multnomah County west to Hillsboro in Washington County, with trains scheduled every 15 minutes during the day to all of downtown, Old Town, the Oregon Zoo, the Lloyd Center, the Rose Quarter, and the airport. MAX has three lines: the Blue Line, which runs east and west between Gresham and Hillsboro via downtown Portland; the Red Line, which runs from the Beaverton Transit Center through downtown to the airport; and the Yellow Line, which travels north and south between downtown and the Expo Center, along Interstate Avenue. Smaller conventional buses and vans now provide service on less-traveled suburban routes, and there is a wheelchair-accessible special service. In 2009, two MAX lines will serve riders traveling from Wilsonville to Beaverton and from Milwaukee to downtown Portland.

Fares—which apply equally to buses, light-rail trains, and streetcars—are based on a geographic zone system: $2.00 for one or two zones and $2.30 for all zones. Fares are good for a one-way trip and are discounted for senior citizens and youth. Children six and younger ride for free. Bus drivers will not give you change, though dollar bills are accepted on the bus. A day ticket ($4.75) can be used on buses, streetcars, and light rail, traveling to all zones, and you can also get discounted fares if you buy weekly or monthly passes. These passes are widely available throughout the city at many drugstores, grocery stores, and bookstores. The TriMet Web site has a comprehensive list of outlets.

Bus routes vary in frequency and how early and how long each bus travels its route, but during peak times on the most traveled routes, buses run at least every 15 minutes if not more often, as do MAX trains. Schedules for individual bus lines and the light-rail lines are free and commonly available at banks, stores, post offices, bookstores, and dozens of other locations, or accessible on the Web at www.trimet.org. All stops are marked by blue and white signs displaying the route numbers of the buses serving that line.

## Streetcars

For the first half of the 20th century, Portlanders used streetcars to get around town. Now Portland has brought them back in order to connect the major Westside business districts. Streetcars now travel a route that extends from the South Waterfront district on the Willamette, through Portland State University north to Good Samaritan Hospital (between Northwest Lovejoy and Northwest Northrup at Northwest

23rd), traveling through the Pearl District and along 10th and 11th Avenues. This means you can drive downtown for shopping, then hop on a streetcar to visit Powell's City of Books at 10th and Burnside before your lunch reservation in the Pearl District, all without having to move your car.

Like the bus, streetcars stop every 2 to 3 blocks, and they run from 5:30 a.m. to 11:00 p.m. Monday through Thursday and until 11:45 p.m. on Friday. Saturday hours are from 7:15 a.m. to 11:45 p.m. and Sunday from 7:15 a.m. to 10:30 p.m. They arrive every 12 to 15 minutes during peak hours and a bit less frequently at other times. Well-marked, glass-covered streetcar stops, however, are equipped with electronic screens that helpfully note when the next streetcar will arrive.

Fares follow the same schedule as the MAX and the bus, and their tickets and transfers are all interchangeable. To pay your fare, deposit exact change in the farebox when you board. Fareboxes take only $1 and $5 bills and coins. If you've bought tickets elsewhere, simply validate the ticket once on board. (Riding within the Fareless Square is still free.) While the streetcar may be an old-fashioned form of transportation, these are thoroughly modern, with air conditioning, low-floor center sections, and full wheelchair access. They are clean and efficient.

Those with a nostalgic bent can still ride an old-fashioned streetcar. The Vintage Trolley, a trolley operation using replicas of the streetcars that once served the city, runs on Sunday from March through December. For more information check TriMet's useful Web site at www.trimet.org, which includes an itinerary of historic buildings that the trolley passes as it travels along. The Vintage Trolley charges no fare but welcomes donations.

## By Tram

To ride the Portland Aerial Tram: Tickets are purchased from a kiosk at the lower terminal at OHSU's Center for Health and Healing. (This outpatient facility

also has an excellent cafe and coffee bar, just so you know.) Tickets cost $4, though children ages 6 and under ride for free, as do patients, visitors, and employees of OHSU (including Doernbecher Children's Hospital). The ticket kiosk takes coins and credit or debit cards, but not bills. Tickets are collected only on the way up, but all tickets are round-trip. If you are a patient or visitor, you will need to get a pass from your provider. If you have a monthly TriMet pass or annual streetcar pass, you can ride for free as well, but ordinary TriMet transfer passes are not accepted. The ride takes about three minutes, or a bit longer if it is windy. The tram operates

**i** Try the Portland Visitors Association Web site for deals on hotel rooms and help with planning your trip: www.travel portland.com.

weekdays from 5:30 a.m. to 9:30 p.m., on Saturday from 9:00 a.m. to 5:00 p.m., and on Sunday from mid-May through mid-September from 1:00 to 5:00 p.m. It's closed on legal holidays. The tram departs about every 10 minutes. For the latest info, be sure to check the tram Web site, www.portlandtram.org.

Taxis

Portland, Oregon, isn't New York City or Washington, D.C., where taxis are a way of urban life. Good luck trying to flag one from the corner: They will rarely, if ever, stop. However, you can telephone for one. If you're walking around downtown, the best cab-finding solution is to head to a hotel and have the doorperson call a cab. If you're at a restaurant, the maitre d' will usually call one for you. If you know your plans for a specific trip or destination, phone ahead and schedule a cab. Fares start at $2.50 and go up $2.20 per mile—though that could increase as the price of oil increases.

# Accommodations

Visitors to Portland will find a variety of motel and hotel offerings, from the basic to the sublime. They range in style, in price, and in location, but no matter where you plan to stay, you should be able to find a place to lay your head and suit your needs. You will find certain chains well represented throughout the Portland Metro area. For example, Marriott's Courtyard, Fairfield Inns, and Residence Inns, offering consistently clean and comfortable rooms, can be found in Beaverton, Southeast Portland, Hillsboro, Tigard, downtown, the Lloyd Center, North Portland, at the airport, and at other hubs. So can the Homewood Suites and the Garden Inns by the Hilton chain, Holiday Inn Express, Phoenix Inns, Ramada Inns, and many other well-known chains. We figure you know about these reliable places already, so in this guide we have concentrated on the standouts in the area. Many of the hotels listed here have excellent deals if you book them online, so be sure to look at their Web sites.

Not surprisingly, it is expensive to park your car downtown, where hotels charge about $30 per day. Some hotels do offer free parking for guests. Some provide valet parking at their own facilities or nearby garages; others offer their guests discounted parking at local garages.

## Price Code

The following price code for hotels, motels, and bed-and-breakfasts in this chapter is based on an average room rate for double occupancy during high season. While there is no sales tax in Oregon, there is a room tax of 12.5 percent.

| | |
|---|---|
| $ | $60 and less |
| $$ | $61–$110 |
| $$$ | $111–$160 |
| $$$$ | $161 and above |

Please note that many hotels and motels change their room rates at least twice a year, so the ranges we have quoted in this chapter are meant simply as a guide to point you in the right direction, not as the final word on the cost of your stay.

## *Southwest Portland*

**Ace Hotel**                    $$
1022 Southwest Stark St.
(503) 228-2277
www.acehotel.com

The Ace is very Portland, with an indie aesthetic and an attitude to match. The 79 rooms vary widely in standards of luxury—some are private and others share baths and some even have bunk beds designed to house touring bands.

Local artists were hired to create murals throughout the hotel, but it's not just the artwork that is soulful. Even the business center on the mezzanine radiates West Coast hip, providing MacBooks around a large table. The Ace Hotel is not for everyone. You should be forewarned that it is going for something other than the standard hotel experience (you will not find free coffee or newspapers). An ideal hotel for a weekend getaway with friends, especially since its common spaces are so enticing and its location so central.

### The Benson Hotel $$$$
309 Southwest Broadway
(503) 228-2000, (888) 523-6766
www.bensonhotel.com

A grand and historic Portland building, the Benson has been the hotel of choice for visiting U.S. presidents and other dignitaries since 1912. A commitment to superior quality remains today. The 287 guest rooms and suites are spacious, amply furnished in a traditional style with pleasing modern touches. Its downtown location is convenient to galleries, theaters, restaurants, and shopping. Even if you don't stay here, drop by the lobby bar for a drink. The hotel's London Grill restaurant has been a Portland favorite for generations.

### The Governor Hotel $$$–$$$$
614 Southwest 11th Ave.
(503) 224-3400, (800) 554-3456
www.govhotel.com

The historic Governor is an inviting luxury hotel rooted in the past yet offering every modern convenience. The beautiful stained-glass dome in the adjacent restaurant captures the grandeur of the building, which is a National Historic Landmark. A well-executed historic restoration extends throughout the hotel, including the 100 guest rooms. You'll find a Starbucks in the lobby, and just outside the door is the Portland Streetcar line. The Governor is ideally situated close to downtown shops, galleries, and restaurants. Jake's Bar and Grill, a younger sibling of the original Jake's, one of Portland's oldest and most popular restaurants, is adjacent.

## The Heathman Hotel $$$$
1001 Southwest Broadway at Southwest Salmon St.
(503) 241-4100, (800) 551-0011
www.heathmanhotel.com

This popular and elegant downtown hotel is in a superb location next to Portland's Performing Arts Center and within a few blocks of the Portland Art Museum and the Park Blocks. Known for its attention to detail and its outstanding restaurant, the Heathman Hotel is also distinguished for its collection of work by local and regional artists and by such contemporary American artists as Andy Warhol. The 150 rooms offer a complete array of luxury-hotel amenities. Tea is served every afternoon (reservations strongly suggested) in the Tea Court Lounge.

ℹ Even if you're not staying in them, Portland's beautiful downtown hotels are good places to visit. The Marble Bar at the Heathman, the lounge at the Benson, and the bar at the Ace Hotel are but a few of the agreeable spots to while away an hour before dinner.

**Hotel deLuxe Portland**　　$$$–$$$$
729 Southwest 15th Ave.
(503) 219-2094, (866) 895-2094
www.hoteldeluxeportland.com

A stylish hotel that lies just south of the Pearl District, west of downtown and off the MAX line very near PGE Park, so it is convenient to everything. The hotel's decor pays homage to the era of the classic studio films, with stills from memorable movie moments lining the corridors and coolly elegant rooms. But its amenities are strictly 21st century (flat-screen HDTVs adorn each room). Be sure to check out the hotel bar, The Driftwood Room—a fine spot for a pre-dinner cocktail.

**Hotel Fifty**　　$$–$$$
50 Southwest Morrison St.
(503) 221-0711, (877) 505-7220
www.hotelfifty.com/index.php

This urbane and contemporary spot quite near the Willamette River is a lovingly upgraded and refurbished hotel that offers excellent value and an outstanding location. Hotel Fifty will provide you with the standard amenities of a modern hotel, including free wireless, snug memory foam beds and cool linens, iPod docks, and large, capacious showers. In addition, all rooms are non-smoking. Parking is $20 per day, but the hotel is very, very close to the MAX line, so in theory you don't need a car. One nice touch is that they will let you print your boarding pass without having to pay all the excessive business-center charges that hotels like to add. In addition, they have a really decent small conference room, and tech support is available for those gnarly conference call issues. Another amenity, H50, is not some random oxygen species, but is in fact a nice bistro that is perfectly suited for its location.

### The Hotel Lucia $$$–$$$$
400 Southwest Broadway
(503) 225-1717, (877) 225-1717
www.hotellucia.com

The comfortable, well-designed Lucia is well located at the northern edge of the heart of downtown, close to all the major business, tourist, and shopping districts. The Lucia pays close attention to detail and thoughtfully provides pillowtop mattresses and plush robes, flat screen televisions, iPod docks, and high-speed wireless Internet access (for a daily fee) in its 128 rooms. The hotel's restaurant features an outstanding Thai menu that

is also available for room service. The Lucia features a permanent collection of the photographs of David Kennerly, the Pulitzer Prize–winning Oregonian.

**Hotel Modera** $$–$$$$
515 Southwest Clay St.
(503) 484-1084
www.hotelmodera.com

The guests of the Hotel Modera are lucky pilgrims to this sleek temple of West Coast cool. With the confident air of a yoga instructor, the hotel guides its guests in how to be in Portland. It offers a number of room options—multiroom suites as well as singles—and fantastic Internet specials; we recommend checking their Web site directly for the best deals. Free passes to 24-Hour Fitness down the street are also yours for the asking. And they thoughtfully provide parking ($27 per night) in their secured garage, though the hotel is also within easy, easy walking distance to the MAX and the streetcar. The best part of the Hotel Modera is the large courtyard—a testament to urban landscape design, with a living wall and fire pits. What could be better than a summer evening in a high-design courtyard with a cocktail, a loved one, and a fire pit right in the heart of downtown Portland?

**Hotel Monaco** $$$$
506 Southwest Washington St.
(503) 222-0001, (888) 207-2201
www.monaco-portland.com

Rooms at the Hotel Monaco (which is listed in the National Register of Historic Places) are like French salons, decorated in creamy tones, eclectic furniture, and opulent linens. There are 229 rooms, and each includes 32-inch plasma televisions, speaker phones and voice mail, and Wi-Fi. The Red Star Tavern and Roast House is one of Portland's best. Guests are just a block from Pioneer Courthouse Square. Stations for the MAX going both east and west are also very close. Shopping, museums, the Performing Arts Center, and a host of excellent restaurants are nearby.

## Hotel Vintage Plaza $$$–$$$$

422 Southwest Broadway
(503) 228-1212, (800) 263-2305
www.vintageplaza.com

The Plaza features a wine country theme that extends to the names of most rooms, the interior color scheme, and a nightly tasting of Oregon wines at the lobby fireplace. The rooms are private, warm, comfortable, and tasteful. All aspects of the hotel's service are personal and highly polished. There are "starlight rooms" with conservatory windows that let natural light flow into the room and some two-story townhouse suites. Pazzo Ristorante occupies the ground floor; its Northern Italian cuisine touched by Northwest influences is popular with locals. The hotel, on the north end of downtown, is close to major shopping, cultural, and business districts.

### The Mark Spencer Hotel      $$–$$$
409 Southwest 11th Ave.
(503) 224-3293, (800) 548-3934
www.markspencer.com

The Mark Spencer is a particularly good choice for extended stays in Portland. Perhaps more modest and conservative than some of the newer and trendier downtown hotels, the Mark Spencer's location offers convenience and value in its 101 rooms and suites. Afternoon tea is served daily in the lobby. The Mark Spencer is just across Burnside Street from Powell's City of Books and close to both the MAX and streetcar lines.

### The Nines      $$–$$$$
525 Southwest Morrison
(503) 222-999
www.thenines.com

The Nines is a gorgeous hotel, balancing its historic exterior with a lovely, modern interior that provides the expected amenities of a luxury operation, such as a VIP floor, spacious and comfortable rooms, and cozy beds and soft linens. It is part of the Starwood chain, and in spite of its luxury status, it offers great value (there are many Internet specials). It is incredibly convenient to stay here— the MAX line from the airport stops right across the street. The Nines has several restaurants, lounges, and bars.

**The Paramount Hotel**  $$$$
808 Southwest Taylor St.
(503) 223-9900, (800) 716-6199
www.portlandparamount.com

The 154 rooms at this European-style hotel are chic, comfortable, and bigger than what you'll find in most hotels, with added luxuries such as granite bathrooms. Some rooms come with terraces and jetted tubs. The stylish restaurant and bar, the Dragonfish Asian Cafe, provides room service. The downtown location could not be more central.

**The Westin Portland**  $$$$
750 Southwest Alder St.
(503) 294-9000
www.starwoodhotels.com

One of the nicest downtown luxury hotels, the Westin imparts the feeling that its guests are the most important creatures in the world with the lushness of its surroundings and the attentiveness of its service. The rooms are elegant, with cozy down duvets on the beds and oversize, walk-in showers in the bathrooms. The Daily Grill restaurant serves attentively prepared American cuisine.

### Northwest Portland
**Inn at Northrup Station**  $$$
2025 Northwest Northrup St.
(503) 224-0543, (800) 224-1180
www.northrupstation.com

A stylish hotel featuring suites that balance a hip aesthetic with contemporary comforts. Its rooms are brightly colored and filled with modern furniture and dramatic marble and granite in the bathrooms and kitchens. Northrup Station is well located between the lively shopping and restaurant districts on Northwest 21st and Northwest 23rd Avenues—and it's right on the streetcar line, offering easy access to the Pearl District and downtown Portland.

**Jupiter Hotel**                    $$
800 East Burnside St.
(503) 230-9200, (877) 800-0004
www.jupiterhotel.com

The Jupiter is at the center of the revival of "LoBu"—Lower Burnside, on the east side of the Willamette River. It is a restyled motel built in the 1960s and evokes that

era's Land-of-Tomorrow, modern sensibility. Its 80 rooms are divided into the "quiet" side and the "party" side, which is important information depending on how you view proximity to the adjacent Doug Fir Lounge (one of Portland's hottest night spots). As the apotheosis of hip Portland, it's where the Beautiful People stay.

**McMenamins Kennedy School**        **$$**
5736 Northeast 33rd Ave.
(503) 249-3983, (888) 249-3983
www.mcmenamins.com/Kennedy

The wonderful Kennedy School is a favorite recommendation for out-of-town guests. This unusual 35-room inn inhabits a pretty ex-school (now on the Historic Register), reclaiming classrooms and offices to provide comfortable and spacious rooms for guests. The rooms are charmingly decorated with rich colors and cozy, vintage furniture. The inn is far more than a guesthouse. This extensive campus is frequented by Portland residents, as there are excellent bars, a brewery, restaurants, and theaters (for both movies and live music). This place is quintessential Portland.

### Outlying Areas
**McMenamins Edgefield**        **$–$$**
2126 Southwest Halsey St., Troutdale
(503) 669-8610, (800) 669-8610
www.mcmenamins.com/Edge

Like the Kennedy School (see earlier), Edgefield is a reclaimed historic building. It is a big complex that includes a variety of operations besides a hostelry. A large McMenamins' brewery is on the grounds, and it is also the home of the McMenamin brothers' winery. In the main lodge is the Black Rabbit Restaurant and Bar, and you will also find the Power Station Pub and Theater, Loading Dock Beer Garden and Grill, the Little Red Shed (a bar that serves the hard stuff and offers cigars), and the Ice House, which possesses the only television on the grounds (rooms are free of phones as well). Rooms are spacious and handsome, but this is a hotel in the European style—which is to say that most of its 100 rooms are served by bathrooms that serve the whole wing.

Several rooms with private baths are available.

### North/Northeast Portland
**The Blue Plum**                          $$–$$$
2026 Northeast 15th Ave.
(503) 288-3848, (877) 288-3844
www.bluepluminn.com

This handsome inn in the Irvington district was built in 1900. It offers four rooms with private baths, some of which can be combined into suites. A major attraction of the Blue Plum, however, is the attentively prepared breakfasts that feature fresh Northwest ingredients. The vintage furnishings disguise the modern amenities such as wireless Internet access. The location is excellent—the beautiful neighborhood is a pleasure for walking, and the inn is very close to the shops and restaurants of Broadway, the Lloyd Center shopping mall, and the Oregon Convention Center.

### Portland's White House $$$
1914 Northeast 22nd Ave.
(503) 287-7131, (800) 272-7131
www.portlandswhitehouse.com

Completely restored to the grand splendor of 1911, this hotel was built of Honduran mahogany. It has nine elegant guest rooms, all with private baths and featuring period furnishings and decor. The inn is a local landmark, close to attractions on the city's East Side and convenient to downtown. A chef's breakfast by candlelight includes a signature dish: salmon eggs Benedict with orange hollandaise. Children are welcome if you arrange it in advance.

# Restaurants

The Pacific Northwest has long been known for its regional abundance. Modern chefs in Portland carry on a long tradition of using regional ingredients and preparing them in clever ways. The Willamette Valley provides some of the most fruitful farmland in the nation, and we also have a mild climate with a decently long growing season. For a city of our size, we have an outsize reputation as a food mecca, a reputation that grows daily. As the *New York Times* recently noted, Portland is enjoying "a golden age of dining and drinking." Which raises the question of what you should drink with all this bounty. The region is known especially for its excellent wine and beer, its fine coffee roasters and tea houses. We share the climate of the Burgundy region of France, and many of the varietal grapes that grow well there also grow well here. Hops—the ingredient that gives beer its piquancy—also grow well here.

## Price Code

Most restaurants have offerings at a range of prices. The price code here reflects the general cost of a single entree, excluding drinks, hors d'oeuvres, side dishes, and tips. As with other Portland purchases, there is no sales tax.

| | |
|---|---|
| $ | **$10 or less** |
| $$ | **$11–$20** |
| $$$ | **$21–$30** |
| $$$$ | **More than $30** |

## Southwest Portland

**Clyde Common**                    $$
1014 Southwest Stark St.
(503) 228-3333

The signature restaurant of the Ace Hotel, Clyde Common is a stylish space that attracts the beautiful people of Portland to its handsome zinc-topped bar and high-ceilinged dining room—a dining room that features communal tables, where you may find yourself sitting next

to the beautiful people. Fortunately, the friendly staff makes sure there is also room for you. The scene, however, could be unbearable if the food weren't first-class. The bar on weekend nights is very festive, so if you need a quiet dinner, you might make another choice.

**Higgins Restaurant and Bar**         $$$$
1239 Southwest Broadway
(503) 222-9070

The inventive ways in which chef Greg Higgins uses seasonal, organic food from nearby farms, forests, and streams have won this handsome downtown restaurant the highest marks from critics—as well as from the customers that fill the restaurant every night. Because the menu is seasonal, it changes all the time; however, diners can always count on at least one vegan dish on the menu in addition to the beef, duck, fish, and other entrees. The bar menu carries some notable staples, among them an incredibly savory hamburger and a luscious pastrami sandwich (Greg Higgins makes the pastrami himself).

### Kenny & Zuke's $$
1038 Southwest Stark St.
(503) 222-3354

This Jewish delicatessen fills a void in Portland, with stellar sandwiches. Signature dishes include the Reuben sandwich, as well as its variety of pastrami sandwiches on housemade rye bread. All of these are delicious. Kenny & Zuke's is also open early and late, a bit of a

mitzvah. You can eat their pastrami from 7:00 a.m. to midnight Tuesday through Thursday, until 3:00 a.m. on Friday and Saturday, and from 8:00 a.m. to 10:30 p.m. on Sunday.

### Southpark $$

901 Southwest Salmon St.
(503) 326-1300

Southpark is evocative of Casablanca—not only in its decor but also in its menu. We like the dining room, where they specialize in using Northwest ingredients—especially seafood—to showcase inventive Mediterranean-inspired dishes. But we like the wine bar even more, with its murals, velvet drapes, and gleaming metallic bar. The wine list is first class, and so is the service.

Southpark is also good for cocktails and people-watching, not so much because it's a scene but because everyone, including the servers, seems to be having such a nice time.

## Northwest Portland

### Andina $$$

1314 Northwest Glisan St.
(503) 228-9535

This stylishly renovated warehouse in the Pearl District is a star in the Portland restaurant scene. Comprising a tapas bar, an aperitif bar, a wine shop, and the capacious dining room, Andina showcases the cuisine of Peru to great effect. It is a beautiful restaurant, both in the space itself and in the presentation of the food. The wine list is well edited; the service at Andina is professional and the servers' knowledge is excellent, which is helpful if you are unfamiliar with Peruvian cuisine. Andina serves lunch Monday through Saturday and dinner every evening.

## Paley's Place $$$$
1204 Northwest 21st Ave.
(503) 243-2403

Paley's Place, run by an amiable couple in Northwest Portland, is justifiably one of Portland's favorite restaurants: Between chef Vitaly Paley's imagination and talent and Kimberly Paley's gregarious command of the dining rooms, Paley's Place offers one of the best meals in town. Here, the simplest ingredients are turned into Northwest-nuanced, French-inspired dishes prepared by a masterful chef. The menu is always changing, but you might find garlicky mussels prepared with hand-cut fries; a beautiful cut of Kobe beef; maple-glazed chicken with Granny Smith apples, sour cherries, and smoky bacon; halibut served with lentils, fennel, and fiddlehead ferns; or sautéed sweetbreads with leek potato gratin and pomegranate sauce. The restaurant, residing in a pretty, old house in Northwest Portland, has only 50 seats. Yet its two dining rooms, bar, and patio convey the feeling of a larger restaurant without losing any intimacy. Paley's is open seven nights a week for dinner only.

## Park Kitchen $$$

422 Northwest 8th Ave.
(503) 223-7275

On the shady and peaceful North Park blocks—just a few steps from the hurly-burly of Broadway—you will find Park Kitchen, a lovely little restaurant that offers an ever-changing menu of super-lative tavern-style cooking. This restau-rant is small, but the west wall opens up to the stately old trees that line the street, providing a wonderful continu-ity between indoors and out. Chef Scott Dolisch is one of Portland's best, and everything here is tempting, beautifully prepared, and chosen with great care.

## Pearl Bakery $

102 Northwest 9th Ave.
(503) 827-0910

Pearl Bakery is one of several excellent artisanal bakeries in town, featuring rus-tic Italian breads as well as breakfast and dessert pastries, but they also operate a tiny cafe. Here you will find a wonderful array of *panini*, focaccia, deli sandwiches, and salads. The sandwich fillings might include roasted eggplant and tomato pesto or fig and anise. The breads are outstanding—traditional sourdoughs are favorites but so are country-style loaves such as levain with green or kala-mata olives. Breakfast pastries include tempting specialties such as apple cof-fee cake and pear Danish.

## Southeast Portland

**Bar Avignon**  $$
2138 Southeast Division St.
(503) 517-0808
baravignon.com

Proprietors Randy Goodman and Nancy Hunt will tell you that Bar Avignon is just a bar, but don't believe them. This sleek and organic spot along Southeast Division offers a beautifully edited wine collection and wonderful spirits that frame an outstanding selection of small plates. These include silky cured meats, creamy cheeses served with honey and Marcona almonds, just-harvested salads, the ripest fruit, the crustiest bread from the Little T bakery up the street—in short, everything you need to make a complete meal for the entire family, provided they are all over 21. The service is attentive and the atmosphere is enlivening, full of attractive and convivial people who are all evidently enjoying themselves. You should join them.

**Biwa**  $$
215 Southeast 9th Ave.
(503) 239-8830

For a city on the Pacific Rim, and considering the number of Japanese language and cultural programs we have, Portland has surprisingly few authentic Japanese restaurants. Fortunately, Biwa has closed this gap. The "small plates"–style emphasizes variety in taste and high-quality ingredients. Standout dishes include the vegetable salad, which features cabbage rolls, carrots, and daikon radish in a silky sesame dressing; pork belly; *onigiri,* little stuffed rice and nori sandwiches; and offerings of two different noodle styles.

## Castagna $$$$
1752 Southeast Hawthorne Blvd.
(503) 231-7373

Castagna is a sophisticated and spare restaurant on the western end of Hawthorne, with a minimalist ambience that allows the food to take center stage. The presentation here is outstanding, and even simple dishes such as a butter lettuce salad, sea scallops, or french fries are beautifully arranged on large white plates. Everything from the white bean soup to the last crumb of bittersweet chocolate tartlet is impressive to both the eye and the palate. There is no place like Castagna in all of Portland. A less formal, and less expensive, cafe right next door, Café Castagna (1758 Southeast Hawthorne Blvd.; 503-231-9959), provides an excellent meal.

## Ken's Artisan Pizza $$
304 Southeast 28th Ave.
(503) 517-9951

Owner Ken Forkish uses a 700-degree oven, a perfect pizza technique, and keeps the menu simple, a combination that leads to incredibly satisfying dinners. Pizzas are also seasonal—in the fall you might find a squash pizza, while spring may bring roasted asparagus—but you can count on a Margherita, with tomato sauce, mozzarella, and basil or even arugula. Other regular toppings involve house-cured pancetta, anchovies, and Italian sausage. But it is the pizza dough that is the main event: perfectly crusty and chewy and balanced.

## Le Pigeon $$$
738 East Burnside St.
(503) 546-8796

Le Pigeon inhabits a small space decorated with old chandeliers and repurposed chairs, and does not take reservations. In spite of these humble trappings, Le Pigeon is one of the most innovative restaurants in Portland today. Chef Gabriel Rucker uses the typical local, seasonal approach, but in completely novel ways. Menus change a lot, but there are some standout regulars—for example, the peanut butter and jelly sandwich with foie gras, served as an appetizer. Duck confit, crispy sweetbreads, and tongue make regular appearances, as do interesting sides such as pickled strawberries or gazpacho with melon. Desserts frequently incorporate foie gras or bacon to accent the silky sweetness of ice cream or the airiness of a profiterole.

## Nuestra Cocina $$
2135 Southeast Division St.
(503) 232-2135

This remarkable restaurant in Southeast Portland serves Mexican food at its finest—not greasy rice and beans, but complex and savory dishes from Mexico's central regions. The service here is both expert and friendly, and the dining room is handsome, with mosaic tiles and accents of wood. But as pleasant as the service and dining room are, the food is what, rightly, should draw you. One warning: The bar area is very, very small, so there are few options for waiting unless it's a summer night and you can chat outside on the sidewalk. It's worth the wait.

### Pok Pok and Whiskey Soda Lounge  $$
3226 Southeast Division St.
(503) 232-1387

Inhabiting a teeny hut and a vintage house on Southeast Division, Pok Pok's modest exterior belies its perfect and authentic Thai cooking. Everything here is delicious, but the major draw is the roasted guinea hens, cooked on a special rotisserie that was imported just for this purpose. They have a gorgeous crispy golden skin, and the juicy meat is infused with lemongrass, garlic, and smoke. Another wonderful dish is the Khao Man Som Tam, a dish of coconut rice, caramelized shredded pork, and fried shallots, but pretty much anything you get will be good.

### Sel Gris  $$$
1852 Southeast Hawthorne Blvd.
(503) 517-7770
www.selgrisrestaurant.com

Sel Gris is a busy, busy little bistro. *Sel gris,*

which means "gray salt" in French—it's actually sea salt—is definitely an inspiration to chef Daniel Mondok, the man behind the bustle. The menu features abundant seafood, prepared with an inspired hand and creative thought, but fish is not the only standout. Indeed, the most interesting dishes are the ones that surprise you, in a good way, such as macaroni and cheese (made with Israeli couscous and mimolette) or braised pork (this time with ginger beer). Sel Gris has a "chef's bar" along its open kitchen, where you can watch Mondok and his line cooks prepare your dinner. The atmosphere is a hip blend of organic and industrial, and if you want to go there, you should call ahead. It's very, very busy.

## Simpatica Dining Hall $$
838 Southeast Ash St. (dining room entrance)
(503) 235-1600

Simpatica Dining Hall represents a national trend in dining—one that got a major boost from experimentation with the genre in Portland—the "Family Supper." Simpatica serves weekend dinners and brunches to small numbers of people who know great food when they taste it and who are happy to commune with their fellow diners. The brunch features their wonderfully prepared meats, as well as traditional dishes such as waffles, biscuits and gravy, and crepes (albeit with inventive fillings such as squash and bacon). Dinners are typically served as a prix fixe menu with several choices. Vegetarians might be happier elsewhere, but for omnivores Simpatica is one of the best meals in town.

**Vindalho** $$

2038 Southeast Clinton St.
(503) 467-4550

Serving exquisite food in the Indian tradition, Vindalho is unlike any other restaurant between Vancouver, British Columbia, and perhaps San Francisco. It displays a proper respect for the flavors and textures of India while at the same time taking advantage of the amazing basic ingredients the Pacific Northwest has to offer. Vindalho offers many traditional foods—naan bread, lamb kofta

(savory meatballs in a Pakistani curry sauce), curry, tandoori chicken, and lamb.

## North/Northeast Portland

**Ciao Vito** $$$

2293 Northeast Alberta St.
(503) 282-5522

Chef Vito DiLullo opened this attractive restaurant to serve his own neighborhood, but over the years it has become a destination dining spot. Ciao Vito serves honest food beautifully prepared at good value, and in this way it feels more like Italy than Oregon. The focus of the menu is traditional Italian fare using Northwest ingredients, but there are always surprises. Even the simplest dishes—the antipasto, for example—are about 20 times better than anything you're likely to get west of Sicily.

## Fife $$$
4440 Northeast Fremont St.
(971) 222-3433

This beautiful restaurant has an atmosphere that manages to be both sophisticated and warm. While primarily a neighborhood place, plenty of upscale followers from all over the city have beaten a path to the door to sample the American cuisine produced by chef Marco Shaw. The menu stars less common meats such as quail, venison, rabbit, and buffalo, as well as silky pork shoulder and tender lamb. Starters have included a wondrous, delicate squash soup, fragrant with cinnamon, as well as Fife's signature crab cakes. Everything is prepared with skill and ingenuity, and the service is poised and professional.

**i** Oregon and Washington are among the vanguard of artisanal cheesemakers, and the Pacific Northwest Cheese Project is dedicated to making sure we know how blessed they are. Find them at http://pnwcheese.typepad.com.

## Lovely Hula Hands $$$
4057 North Mississippi Ave.
(503) 445-9910

The atmosphere is attractive and romantic. You'll find a full bar with expertly prepared cocktails, among them their own signatures such as Talulah's Bathwater, a sticky concoction of pomegranate molasses, tequila, fresh lime, and sugar, as well as the classics. Chef Troy MacLarty's menu is haute Northwest cuisine, contrapuntal in textures and flavors. Salads are outstanding, often combining something savory, such as smoked fish or cheese, with something fruity, such as grapefruit. Entrees are equally delicious. Lovely Hula Hands does not take reservations, but you may want to call ahead if you have a larger group (more than four people).

## Siam Society $$
2703 Northeast Alberta St.
(503) 922-3675

Siam Society serves some of the best Thai food in town—well balanced, exquisitely fresh, and perfectly textured. Though the restaurant has a daily-changing menu, it tends to carry some items all the time, even if fillings or sauces might change. You will find a variety of salads and spring rolls based on what's in season; likewise for the soups. The restaurant occupies a renovated electrical substation and uses this to great effect. Soaring ceilings and tall windows make it feel spacious.

**Toro Bravo** $$

120 Northeast Russell St.
(503) 281-4464

Toro Bravo carries the Spanish flag for Portland restaurants. It truly is a tapas "bar," and the best approach to take there is to order just a few dishes, hang onto the menu, and then order some more. Local favorites include the coppa steak, prepared with spinach and golden raisins; bacon-wrapped dates; scallops; duck rillettes; and grilled chanterelle mushrooms.

# Brewpubs

Portland may have more microbreweries and brewpubs than any city in the nation—over 30 at last count—reflecting a climate hospitable to hops and a fanatic devotion to the homegrown. Our climate is excellent for growing hops (we grow at least 14 varieties) and barley, and beer brewing is a long tradition. Combine these resources with the do-it-yourself ethos left over from Oregon's hippie days, and you have a revolution in the making. Pubs and brewpubs have fast become a way of life for Oregonians, and many of them are very family-friendly, offering simple food and sometimes even craft-brewed root beer. As long as a pub is also a restaurant, most of them will allow children until 10:00 p.m. in designated areas. It is very common to see families in these pubs, so if you want to bring the little ones, don't be shy.

## Southwest Portland
**Full Sail Brewing**
307 Southwest Montgomery St.
(503) 222-5343
www.fullsailbrewing.com

A small operation that makes light, easy-to-sip ales and lagers. Sample one of Full

Sail's brews as you gaze through a glass wall at brewers making a new batch.

## Tugboat Brewing Co.

711 Southwest Ankeny St.
(503) 226-2508

Tugboat likes to make powerful British-style beers, and their many offerings include an Extra Special Bitter and a hoppy India Pale Ale. The owner also repairs watches—the brewery is housed in a historic watch- and clock-repair shop—in case yours has stopped.

### *Northwest Portland*

**Bridgeport Brewpub**

1313 Northwest Marshall St.
(503) 241-3612
www.bridgeportbrew.com

**i** You may find the urge to brew your own, if you stay in Portland long enough. For brewing supplies and expert advice, go to F. H. Steinbart, 234 Southeast 12th Avenue (503-232-8793), or Let's Brew, 9021 Northeast Killingsworth Street (503-256-0205), and they will help you get set up.

The oldest of Portland's craft breweries (est. 1984), house standards include Coho Pacific and the flagship ale, Blue Heron Amber Ale, brewed in honor of Portland's official city bird. Bridgeport also serves up a fine pizza, with dough made fresh daily from unfermented beer wort.

### Deschutes Brewery & Public House
210 Northwest 11th Ave.
(503) 296-4906
www.deschutesbrewery.com

The Deschutes Brewery is known for its outstanding brews such as Mirror Pond Pale Ale, Obsidian Stout, Black Butte Porter, and the Armory XPA (a pale ale). The menu takes the normal pub fare up a notch, with local and organic meats and produce in the delicious burgers, pizzas, and fish and chips.

### New Old Lompoc
1616 Northwest 23rd Ave.
(503) 225-1855

Here you will find powerful beers brewed with great attention to balance. Try the rich Sockeye Cream Stout or the Proletariat Red, both strong beers that warrant total attention.

### Rogue Ales Public House
1339 Northwest Flanders St.
(503) 222-5910

The beers served here include Rogue Red, Brutal Bitter, Buckwheat Ale, Porter, Stout, Rogue Smoke, and Maierbock; some of these are in pressurized kegs.

### *Southeast Portland*
### Hopworks Urban Brewery
2944 Southwest Powell Blvd.
(503) 232-4677
www.hopworksbeer.com

This busy pub brews organic, hand-crafted beer and serves it in four beautiful spaces: an outdoor beer garden, an indoor family space (that includes a play area), a mezzanine, and a bike-up bar. Every inch is devoted to sustainable restaurant practice, from the permeable pavers lining the beer garden to the rain barrels and composting system.

**The Horse Brass Pub**
4534 Southeast Belmont St.
(503) 232-2202
www.horsebrass.com

No visit to Portland is complete without a stop at the Horse Brass for a pint of bitter and a game of darts. This gem of a place is a pub in the finest and truest sense of the word, offering plenty of atmosphere and 46 draughts of the finest microbrewed and imported beers.

### North/Northeast Portland
**Concordia Brewery**
McMenamins Kennedy School
5736 Northeast 33rd Ave.
(503) 249-3983
www.mcmenamins.com/Kennedy

Beers include the usual McMenamin offerings, plus some guests. Much of the beer is brewed on-site. Food offerings are also standard—sandwiches, fries, salads, and other appetizery things, but with more variety in the entree department. For more information on the Kennedy School, see the Accommodations chapter.

### Widmer Brothers Gasthaus
929 North Russell St.
(503) 281-2437
www.widmer.com

The Gasthaus, in an old refurbished 1890s hotel adjacent to the Widmer's brewery, serves a complete menu, ranging from beer and appetizers to full dinners. Widmer Brothers Brewing Company is the top-selling craft brewer in the region and produces seven original European- and Pacific Northwest–style beers.

# Coffeehouses

Portlanders have a well-established tradition of hanging out in coffeehouses that predates Starbucks, so you will find all throughout the city many different kinds of coffeehouse aesthetic, from the sleek urbane to the shabby chic. And the word *coffeehouse* may mean anything from a small espresso bar to a cafe to a combination of tavern and coffeehouse.

Below, we've listed some of the much-loved coffeehouses in the area. We also encourage you to explore for yourself to find your own favorites, because so many good coffeehouses are out there that we could never list them all.

**Coffeehouse Northwest**
1951 West Burnside St.
(503) 248-2133
www.coffeehousenorthwest.com

**Ken's Artisan Bakery**
326 Northwest 21st Ave.
(503) 248-2202

**The Old Nob Hill Pharmacy Cafe**
2100 Northwest Glisan St.
(503) 548-4049

**Stumptown Coffee Roasters**
4525 Southeast Division St.
(503) 230-7702

3356 Southeast Belmont St.
(503) 232-8889
www.stumptowncoffee.com

## North/Northeast Portland

**Albina Press**
4637 North Albina Ave.
(503) 282-5214

**Fresh Pot**
4001 North Mississippi Ave.
(503) 284-8928
www.thefreshpot.com

**Ristretto Roasters**
3520 Northeast 42nd Ave.
(503) 284-6767
www.ristrettoroasters.com

# Attractions

Visitors come from all over to see what makes the Portland area different from other parts of the country and world. This chapter emphasizes the local and regional attractions—natural, historical, and contemporary—that define and characterize our area. Getting to these attractions is usually simple. Most are concentrated within the city center. Downtown Portland, which is encompassed in our Southwest Portland section, is agreeable for walking, and even if the weather is not entirely cooperative, the distances are relatively short. Fareless Square, a downtown zone along the bus mall (in which bus fare is free), invites visitors to join local residents on buses, MAX trains, and streetcars to get around downtown more easily. Visitors to attractions in outlying areas, such as Fort Vancouver, will depend more on cars. You can still take public transportation, but it requires more planning and commitment.

The entire Portland Metro area is an attraction, full of interesting things to watch, do, hear, and taste. During the spring and summer, expect the occasional parade, especially during the Rose Festival and on the Fourth of July, as well as street festivals, bike races, weekend runs, and even the occasional protest outside some government building. We have made every effort to report the most current and accurate hours and addresses. However, given the rate of change in the area, visitors are advised to call their destination beforehand to make sure the information is accurate.

## Southwest Portland

### Hoyt Arboretum

Washington Park
4000 Southwest Fairview Blvd.
(503) 823-7529, (503) 865-8733
www.hoytarboretum.org

Hoyt Arboretum lies within the boundaries of Washington Park. Its 214 forested acres offer unsurpassed arboreal beauty as well as beautiful views of the city, and it's large enough that you can get into some backwoods areas where you aren't bumping into other hikers every time you round a bend in the trail—though it's popular with trail runners, so be careful when rounding those blind corners. Hoyt Arboretum features a collection of conifers, 10 miles of trails, the vestiges of our rural past, and some striking views of the city and the Cascades. We love to take the Fir Trail all the way to the Pittock Mansion. It only takes about 45 minutes, and the view is stunning. (See the listing later in this chapter for more information.)

**International Rose Test Garden**
**400 Southwest Kingston in**
**Washington Park**
**(503) 823-3636**

For some residents and visitors, this park is what Portland is about. High above the city, offering an eastern view of the skyline, the Willamette River and its bridges, the snowcapped peaks of the Cascade Mountains (Mount Hood, Mount St. Helens, Mount Adams, and even Mount Rainier on some days), the Rose Test Garden is an almost obligatory stop for visitors. It's the oldest public rose test garden in the nation. The roses begin to bloom in May and usually reach their peak sometime in June, depending on the weather. Don't be tempted to pick a single stem, no matter how overcome by the passion for possession. There is a $500 fine for picking a flower. There are no admission fees or formal operating hours.

**Japanese Garden**
**611 Southwest Kingston Ave.**
**(503) 223-1321**
**www.japanesegarden.com**

A Japanese ambassador to the United States once commented that this site in

Washington Park is the most beautiful and authentic Japanese garden outside of Japan. The trees and plants, water, and rocks here change with the season, offering visitors different perspectives of color, texture, shape, shadow, and sound throughout the year. In spring, azaleas and flowering cherry trees illuminate the garden. During the summer, flowering shrubs and annuals create dramatic spots of color contrasting with differing tones and shades of green. The varieties of graceful irises provide accents of purple to the garden's green. In fall the garden is aflame with color as the delicate leaves of the Japanese maples turn and brilliantly burst into heated reds and oranges, yellows, and golds. Though the winter months are less flamboyant, these gardens can be restorative to your soul even during the long weeks of gray, damp days. Hours vary according to the season.

## Oregon Historical Society Museum
1200 Southwest Park Ave.
www.ohs.org

The Oregon Historical Society Museum is a fine place to begin a visit to Portland; it covers the history of Oregon from the earliest Indian civilizations through the saga of the Oregon Trail right up to the issues surrounding Portland's light rail. Before you even enter the building, the two eight-story-high trompe l'oeil murals by Richard Haas present dramatic views and symbols of Oregon's past. The West Mural, at Southwest Park Avenue and Madison Street, captures in larger-than-life scale the key members of the Lewis and Clark Expedition including Sacagawea and her child, Baptiste; Clark's slave, York; and Seaman, the dog. The other mural, visible from Broadway and Jefferson Streets, symbolically depicts early Oregon characters, among them Native Americans, trappers, and settlers. There is no cost for children younger than five.

## The Oregon Zoo
4001 Southwest Canyon Rd.
(503) 226-1561
www.oregonzoo.com

The Oregon Zoo is the newest name for a zoo originally established in 1887. It has evolved from a hodgepodge of animals kept at the back of a pharmacy into a world-class research facility, offering a constantly changing mix of exhibits and other amusements. It's an internationally recognized and respected center for breeding Asian elephants, and it features an imaginative re-creation of the African rain forest. It's undergone a significant overhaul and renewal in the past few years, including a major new commitment to educating visitors about the animals of the Pacific Northwest. It continues to make a serious effort to improve the animal habitats. As if in response to a homier atmosphere, the zoo's animal population is remarkably fertile, and the nursery is one of the most popular exhibits with adults, children, and the Portland media.

During the summer, the zoo hosts a series of concerts on a stage surrounded by terraced lawns. Many of these concerts are free with zoo admission; others cost more. The mild evenings, popular artists, and availability of catered food, regional wines and beer, and coffee combine to make these concerts into events that express the very essence of Portland. Many people bring a picnic (you can bring anything edible except alcohol into the zoo) and sprawl on blankets in the late afternoon sunshine before the music begins.

## Pioneer Courthouse
555 Southwest Yamhill St.

Pioneer Courthouse, the second-oldest federal building west of the Mississippi, was Portland's first restoration project back in the 1970s. Built in the late 1860s of beautiful Bellingham sandstone, the Italianate building survived ill-considered plans that would have had it demolished for a mundane office building in the 1930s, for a parking lot in the 1940s, and for a new federal office building in the 1960s. Most of the city's residents don't know it, but you can climb to the cupola of Pioneer Courthouse for a rarely seen view of the city. To reach the cupola, enter the courthouse (not the Post Office on

Southwest 6th Avenue) from Southwest Yamhill Street. Admission is free.

## Pioneer Courthouse Square

**Between Broadway and Southwest
6th Ave. at Southwest Yamhill and
Southwest Morrison Sts.
www.pioneercourthousesquare.org**

Pioneer Courthouse Square has been many things during its long life. The site was home to the city's first public schoolhouse; then home to the Portland Hotel, a massive and impressive building that was torn down, to much local dismay, to make way for a parking lot. Now, however, this wonderful piece of real estate is known as "Portland's living room" for its warm blend of red brick, park benches, flowers, sculpture, and coffee. Look at the bricks in the square's open spaces, and you'll see the inscribed names of more than 64,000 Portland residents, companies, and other Oregonians who paid $25 each to buy the bricks: The citizens of Portland rallied to install this project against some local ill will. (You can still buy a brick, but in these inflationary times, the price has gone up to $100.) Pioneer Square hosts an unending series of special events, including contests, cultural festivals, a giant civic Christmas tree, a yuletide tuba concert, a sand castle contest, officially sanctioned skateboarding competitions, and anything else residents can get approved.

**Pittock Mansion**
3229 Southwest Pittock Dr.
(503) 823-3624
www.pittockmansion.com

Henry Pittock, founder of the *Oregonian,* the city's daily newspaper and the largest paper in the state, built himself a château 1,000 feet above the city. The mansion stayed in the family for 50 years, until 1964, when it was sold to the city of Portland. This 22-room, 16,000-square-foot, antiques- and art-filled house is now open to the public. Guided tours of the house are offered each afternoon, and visitors can wander through the gardens of roses, azaleas, and rhododendrons. In spring, flowering cherry trees add their color to the grounds. The view is spectacular. The adjoining Pittock Acres offer hiking and walking trails and are part of the Audubon Society's Wildlife Preserve.

**Portland Art Museum**
1219 Southwest Park Ave.
(503) 226-2811
www.pam.org

The Portland Art Museum, the oldest museum in the Pacific Northwest, has gained much attention for its major exhibitions and even more major fund-raising capabilities. The results have been impressive: After an extensive expansion, the museum now has the space for new galleries, educational facilities, a multimedia room, an appealing public sculpture garden, and a cafe. This new wealth of space has allowed the museum to better feature its important collections in Northwest and Native American art and in European painting, as well as creating space for recent acquisitions.

**Portland Children's Museum**
Washington Park across from the Oregon Zoo
4015 Southwest Canyon Rd.
(503) 223-6500
www.portlandcm.org

The Portland Children's Museum, which dates from 1949, is especially popular with preschoolers, who adore the high-quality, innovative, and varied play spaces, which range from a child-size grocery store and restaurant to the ingenious waterworks room, where children turn cranks and wind pulleys to rush water through pipes and pools (plastic aprons are provided). Other spaces are devoted to dressing up, to music, and to art. The clay room allows children to pound, roll, and shape real clay. Older children especially like the art workshops, which include pottery painting and the "Garage," a studio for making art out of recycled materials. The museum also offers amusements just for babies, various organized events, and special activities for the holidays.

**Portland Saturday Market**
under the Burnside Bridge on
Southwest 1st Ave.
(503) 222-6072
www.saturdaymarket.org

Since 1974 Saturday Market (it is open on Sunday, too) has been another "must see" for visitors. You can enjoy street theater (some intentional, some not), sample from a range of food booths, and buy everything from candles, macramé, pottery, stained glass, clothing, hemp products, local produce and handmade housewares, furniture and toys, and tools and trinkets. Not as countercultural as they once were, vendors may dress like Deadheads but in reality are small business owners, and there is a fair amount of gray hair and middle-aged spread under the embroidered denim and sandals. Everything is made by hand. The market runs until Christmas. During the holiday-shopping madness,

it is as packed as any department store or mall.

## Tom McCall Waterfront Park
**Bordering Naito Parkway and the Willamette River from Broadway Bridge south to River Place**

If Pioneer Courthouse Square is Portland's living room, the Tom McCall Waterfront Park is the city's front yard. The park starts at the Broadway Bridge, stretches south for about 2 miles, and then converts into a portion of the Greenway, a path continuing south to Willamette Park, a total distance of 3.25 miles. Center stage for Waterfront Park is the Salmon Street Springs Fountain at the foot of Southwest Salmon Street. In hot weather this fountain, with its spurting jets of water, attracts crowds of adults and children who play and splash in the streams of water and the shallow pool. The dock for the *Portland Spirit,* an excursion boat offering cruises on the Willamette, is also nearby. The Waterfront Story Garden, a lighthearted cobblestone and granite monument to storytellers, is one of a small number of memorials. Another is the Japanese American Historical Plaza, sometimes referred to as the Garden of Stones. Across from the Oregon Maritime Museum is the battleship USS *Oregon* monument. The final monument along Waterfront Park is, unfortunately, little noted. In a tribute to the staff of the Canadian Embassy in Tehran, Iran, who helped a number of American diplomats

and their families escape during the year-long Iran Hostage Crisis, a small group of Portlanders commissioned a plaque honoring their bravery.

**Washington Park**
**Southwest Park Place at Southwest**
**Vista Ave.**
**(503) 823-7529**

One of Portland's most popular parks, Washington Park is set on 546 acres on the city's West Hills, where it overlooks downtown Portland and east beyond into the mountains. It is the home of the Oregon Zoo, the World Forestry Center, the Japanese Garden, the Children's Museum, and the Rose Gardens. All these attractions are within walking distance of one another, if you're a sturdy walker. The Oregon Zoo, World Forestry Center, and Children's Museum are right off the MAX stop, and the Japanese and Rose Gardens are about a mile away along the roads or trails of Washington Park. You can also take the zoo train, which has a station at the Rose Gardens, or the TriMet #63 buses that traverse the park and back to town. (You can also take ART the Cultural Bus. ART is a propane-powered bus painted by Henk Pander, one of Portland's best-known artists.)

## *Northwest Portland*
**Portland Classical Chinese Garden**
Northwest 3rd Ave. and Everett St.
(503) 228-8131
www.portlandchinesegarden.org

The exquisite Portland Classical Chinese Garden, more formally known as the "Garden of Awakening Orchids," is a double-walled oasis built in a traditional Chinese style with extensive help from Portland's Chinese sister city Suzhou. It inhabits a city block at the north end of Chinatown and serves as a retreat from the chaos of urban life. But it's more than a retreat. The garden integrates the elements of water, stone, light, shadow, color, texture, and fragrance to form an enclosed small world that mysteriously feels as though it unfurls the entire universe within its walls. The Chinese Garden is meant to inspire you to think about this paradox and others like it. For the scholars who possessed them—scholars who today would be bureaucrats or businessmen—gardens were places of freedom from the pressure and constraints of official life, where their owners could meditate upon the paradoxes of the freedom found in duty or the nature found in culture. One reason the Chinese Garden is powerful is that such paradoxes are not foreign to us moderns. We buy cars and houses in order to be free but then must slave away to pay for the houses and cars. It is easy to enjoy the garden on your own, but if you want to learn more about its history, traditions, and symbolism, we strongly recommend taking one of the tours. Visit the Web site for more information.

### Southeast Portland
### Crystal Springs Rhododendron Garden
Southeast 28th Ave.
(1 block north of Woodstock Blvd.)
(503) 823-3640

Long periods of gray days create a great appreciation for color in many Oregonians. You can see this in the well-tended public and private gardens that celebrate the coming of spring and summer with tulips, lilacs, daffodils, azaleas, magnolias, roses, and rhododendrons. Beginning in April, Oregonians flock to the seven-acre Crystal Springs Rhododendron Garden to savor the brilliant colors of the garden's 2,500 rhododendrons, azaleas, and other plants. While spring is prime time here, the gardens are a delight at any time of the year. In the fall, the Japanese maples and sourwood trees burst into flame, a defiant gesture against the coming monotones of winter. A spring-fed lake attracts a permanent colony of ducks and other waterfowl, not to mention the area's population of birders. Even when the seasons' colors have peaked, the garden attracts visitors looking for solitude and a temporary respite from urban life. From the first of March through Labor Day, on Tuesday and Wednesday, admission fees are waived. Adult admission is $3 the rest of the time. Children are always free. The park is open from dawn to dusk.

### Oregon Museum of Science and Industry (OMSI)

1945 Southeast Water Ave.
(503) 797-6674
www.omsi.edu

One of the most popular attractions in Oregon and one of the five largest science museums in the nation, the Oregon Museum of Science and Industry is really a series of very different exhibits and elements. OMSI is a hands-on museum where visitors, especially children, are encouraged to touch things, try experiments, and question why things happen. Adults and children alike will enjoy the presentations in the large-screen OMNIMAX theater and the variety of programs in the Murdock Sky Theater, a domed theater for programs on astronomy. The core of the museum is a series of specialized exhibit halls, each with a different emphasis and exhibits. While there is a separate admission charge for the USS *Blueback*, the U.S. Navy's last diesel-powered submarine, visitors should not miss a tour of this vessel. This is a real submarine, with confined spaces, no windows, and no onboard restrooms; access is by ladders instead of stairs. Children must be at least four years old and 36 inches tall to tour the submarine.

# Nightlife and Entertainment

Whatever the season, Portland's nightlife is rich and varied. Portland's scene is impossible to pigeonhole—we are not, for example, readily associated with a particular kind of music—but one thing is certain. We love parties; we love our many Waterfront Park festivals; we love those concerts at the zoo. We have a lot to celebrate.

## Basketball

**The Portland Trailblazers**
**The Rose Garden, 1 Center Court**
**(503) 234-9291**
**(503) 321-3211 (events hotline)**
**www.nba.com/blazers**

The Portland Trailblazers—who play in the Western Division of the National Basketball Association—are beloved by Portlanders. The Rose Garden, with seats going from $20 (bring your own oxygen) to more than $145, is one of the best places to be a spectator. It's a great show, with the BlazerDancers swooshing about and many events for the audience. The Rose Garden's 32 public restrooms do have piped-in radio for play-by-play updates, and there are 700 television monitors so you can watch the game while waiting in line for your gardenburger and local brew. Ordinary tickets are usually available even on game day, depending on the opponent. You can often find refreshments-plus-tickets deals and other promotions, too. Tickets are available from the Rose Garden box office and from Ticketmaster, (503) 224-4400, which is also partially owned by Paul Allen. The Blazers' season begins in October; when it ends depends on their skill, luck, opponents, and other playoff-related criteria. If you go to a game, be prepared to pay a lot for parking. Consider parking and riding: MAX runs to within 100 yards of the Rose Garden, and TriMet may eventually figure out, as BART did in San Francisco and Oakland, that they should put on extra trains the nights the Blazers play.

### Southwest Portland

Nightclubs, Dancing, and Live Music

**Berbati's Pan**
**231 Southwest Ankeny St.**
**(503) 248-4579**
**www.berbatis.com**

A big L-shaped dance club connected to a Greek restaurant that serves ethnic food in the bar section, this venerable venue has three hard liquor bars and a stage that hosts a variety of action, from alternative rock concerts to jazz gigs to open-mike comedy to swing dance lessons to Songwriters in the Round. Cover charges range from $6 to $20.

## Bettie Ford Lounge

1135 Southwest Washington St.
(503) 445-8331

A sleek, modernist, downtown club, the Bettie Ford Lounge offers "Cocktail Therapy and Food Late"—as well as R & B, hip-hop, '80s music, and other funky beats to help you dance your troubles away. Join the scenesters and beautiful people at Bettie Ford's three bars, all of which serve tasty, tasty drinks. Cover varies.

**i** Two great bars for Celtic—and other—music are Kells, a handsome bar at 112 Southwest Second Avenue, and the Dublin Pub, a cozy place at 6821 Southwest Beaverton-Hillsdale Highway.

## Crystal Ballroom

1332 West Burnside St.
(503) 225-0047
www.danceonair.com

The Crystal Ballroom is a renovated dance hall with a floating floor on ball bearings and rockers. The dance floor has a capacity for 1,500. Live bands play throughout the week, and Sunday brings ballroom dance lessons to the public. The dress code ranges from jeans and T-shirt to black cocktail dress or three-piece suit. There are a couple of bars serving microbrews and mixed drinks.

## Dante's

1 Southwest 3rd Ave.
(503) 226-6630
www.danteslive.com

Dante's is one of the hottest scenes in downtown Portland—literally. Not only does it have a fiery oil drum to give the place a purgatorial glow, it also attracts a wildly diverse crowd. Could it be the exotic dancers? The expertly mixed cocktails? No—it's the great shows, from the American-Idol fantasists on Monday's karaoke night to the powerful duo Black Angel, who perform Thursday. Other nights are equally spectacular. Dante's is open Monday through Friday from 11:00 a.m. to 2:00 a.m. and on Saturday and Sunday from 7:00 p.m. to 2:00 a.m. The

**i** When you want an old-fashioned cocktail, visit the Marble Bar at the Heathman Hotel to drink in the glamour of an earlier era. Wilf's, at Union Station, serves nightcaps with vintage charm. And the Space Room (4800 Southeast Hawthorne) is perfect when you're feeling more George Jetson than Cary Grant.

club offers a late-night Italian-American menu.

## Embers

110 Northwest Broadway
(503) 222-3082

Embers is a gay dance club that practices tolerance by letting anyone in. With its three stages, it's a great place for dancing, and the music is a fun blend of retro, dance-party, and Top 40. Drag shows are a reliable feature of any night at the Embers. The bar alone is worth a visit.

## Ohm

**31 Northwest 1st Ave.**
**(under the Burnside Bridge)**
**(503) 223-9919**

Ohm is not just a dance club featuring electronica, it's the only dance club featuring electronica that also has a meditation pool on the patio. Ohm adds film, spoken word, and live music to its mix, too—it's an inventive place and a good night out.

## Roseland Theatre and Grill

**8 Northwest 6th Ave.**
**(503) 224-2038**

The Roseland Theatre and Grill is a pleasant all-ages concert pavilion with a bar and roomy balcony upstairs for those over 21. The bill of fare is an eclectic mix of national music and comedy acts, local groups' CD release parties, and DJ dance boogies. A bonus is the emergence of the Roseland Grill downstairs. This narrow slot of a bar has a festive wall covered with posters from the long history of the Roseland.

## Vault

**226 Northwest 12th Ave.**
**(503) 224-4909**
**www.vault-martini.com**

Signature habanero martinis and other frosty concoctions keep the well-clad patrons of this Pearl District hangout returning. Vault has millions of martinis (okay, 44) to choose from, as well as a long list of other cocktails. The ambience is upscale modern, with the work of local artists festooning the walls, a fireplace, and an 18-foot glass bar.

### Southeast Portland
Nightclubs, Dancing, and Live Music
**Aladdin Theater**
3017 Southeast Milwaukie Ave.
(503) 233-1994
www.showman.com

This place lands all kinds of top-drawer acts from many different cultures in and outside of the United States. Aladdin's focus is eclectic: They feature everything from grunge to polka music to classical and neo-country. Once infamous for its record-breaking extended showing of the X-rated film *Deep Throat,* the Aladdin Theater is now famous for blurring the edges between musical genres and is the new darling of Portland's liberal-minded music scene. This place isn't just trendy, it's solid and innovative. Besides snagging some huge and widely respected talent, the Aladdin also books some terrific and often-overlooked artists. Tickets are available daily at the box office out front from 1:00 to 6:00 p.m. and just before the show.

### Blue Monk

3341 Southeast Belmont St.
(503) 595-0575

The Blue Monk is a newer venue for an old favorite: live jazz. They also show jazz movies. The food is Italian, but the atmosphere is decidedly American Urban. Upstairs is a fetching contemporary room with an open kitchen, where cooks are busy preparing steamed mussels, ravioli, or polenta. Downstairs, Portland's finest jazz musicians are jamming.

### Doug Fir

830 East Burnside St.
(503) 231-9663

The local epicenter of Portland nightlife, Doug Fir looks like a mountain lodge that has been given a makeover by Danish modernists. One reason for its popularity: the soft, indirect lighting makes everyone look as if they ought to be carded. The food is really good, but the big draw is the club, which is downstairs. This space features some great bands from all over.

### Holocene

1001 Southeast Morrison St.
(503) 239-7639
www.holocene.org

Holocene is dedicated to the avant-garde of the Portland art and music scene, with an uber-modern interior, two large rooms, and a huge bar. Excellent dancing can be had here, as well as similar music experiences—secret shows by famous artists, up-and-coming bands that will be famous shortly, and other attractions keep hipsters crowding the place.

## Laurelthirst Public House
2958 Northeast Glisan St.
(503) 232-1504

For the alternative folk music crowd, this is a premier nightspot. They've built a great place with a talented and creative kitchen, a variety of microbrews, and a good wine selection. They also draw some of Portland's most sought-after musicians and showcase some terrific and largely unknown talent during open-mike nights.

## Mississippi Studios
3939 North Mississippi Ave.
(503) 753-4473
www.mississippistudios.com

Part recording studio, part concert venue, Mississippi Studios attracts artists from all over to their excellent space. Here, musicians such as Kristin Hersh, Rickie Lee Jones, John Gorka, and Freedy Johnston have all recorded or performed or both. It's a great place to see a show, with a beautiful outdoor garden, bistro, and bar adjacent (called Mississippi Station).

## Vendetta
4306 North Williams Ave.
(503) 288-1085
www.barvendetta.com

A bar with an old-fashioned sense of hospitality, Vendetta not only has a great happy hour and an attractive patio area, but it also has a cool shuffleboard table and live music. A fun neighborhood bar in a fun neighborhood.

## Pool

**Rialto Poolroom, Bar & Cafe**
**529 Southwest 4th Ave.**
**(503) 228-7605**

Minnesota Fats would have felt at home in this downtown pool hall with its 15 full-size Brunswick tables, full bar, sumptuous menu, and downstairs off-track betting. In fact, a photo of Jackie Gleason portraying the legendary stick-man in *The Hustler* is prominently displayed in the bar. Open every day of the year, the Rialto offers a rack of balls and a long stretch of green for $5 an hour before 5:00 p.m. and $7 per hour afterward. If hoisting a cue for a couple of rounds stirs your appetite, try their potato skins with sour cream, bacon, and scallions or their grilled halibut dinner. If you're a vegetarian still yearning for something on a bun, try the gardenburger, one of Portland's hometown products that has spread to many of the nation's supermarkets.

# Shopping

No sales tax in Oregon. What else do you need to know? All right, we'll tell you more. Barn, Banana Republic, and so on—but also many interesting, chic, and homegrown shops. Portland's shopping is organized around its neighborhoods. Portland has other unusual shopping opportunities. Portland Saturday Market, which takes place every weekend under the Burnside Bridge, offers some of the most engrossing shopping in town; it's a carnival of commerce from March through December. For more information see the Attractions chapter or phone (503) 222-6072.

The soul of Portland shopping can be found in its shopping districts. Because the city organizes itself around its neighborhoods, the shopping and business districts play a vital role in creating neighborhood identity and atmosphere. It is possible to find neighborhood shopping so compelling and comprehensive that you won't want to leave your own turf. But that would be a mistake, because the variety of shopping districts gives insight into the character of Portland.

### *Southwest Portland*

Downtown

Department stores, fashionable boutiques, and Pioneer Place, a pedestrian mall, are the highlights of downtown shopping. **Nordstrom,** 701 Southwest Broadway, needs no introduction; this downtown branch flanks the west side of Pioneer Courthouse Square and furnishes area residents with stylish clothes, shoes, and accessories. **Saks Fifth Avenue,** 850 Southwest 5th Avenue, carries beautiful clothing and accessories for men and women (and note—it's actually on 5th Avenue). On the north end of downtown, across Burnside from Powell's City of Books, you'll find cutting-edge bookstores, resale and vintage shops, and record stores. **Reading Frenzy,** 921 Southwest Oak, is especially striking—its collection of alternative periodicals is unparalleled. And on the other end of downtown, the **Oregon Historical Society,** 1200 Southwest Park, has an excellent museum store that provides artwork, books, jewelry, gifts, and other Oregon-related items. **Johnny Sole,** 815 Southwest Alder, purveys Kenneth Cole shoes, Doc Martens, and other stylish footwear for

**i** Many downtown merchants will validate your Smart Park parking slips if you spend $25 or more at their shops. It never hurts to ask.

damp Oregon weather. More downtown enticements include a large **Williams-Sonoma** at 5th and Morrison; **Kathleen's of Dublin,** 737 Southwest Salmon, for beautiful Celtic clothing, jewelry, china, and gifts; **Finnegan's,** 922 Southwest Yamhill, for toys and gifts; **Jane's Vanity,** 521 Southwest Broadway, for alluring underthings; and **Mercantile,** 735 Southwest Park, for upscale women's clothing. **Odessa,** 410 Southwest 13th Avenue carries chic clothes from Kerry Cassill and Mayle, while **Mario's,** 833 Southwest Broadway, equips male and female Portlanders with Prada, Armani, Helmut Lang, and other top designers. (Repeat after me: No sales tax in Oregon.)

**Pioneer Place**
**Southwest Morrison St., between 5th Ave. and 3rd Ave.**
**(503) 228-5800**

Pioneer Place is the epicenter of shopping in downtown, with more than 80 different stores, including the only Saks Fifth Avenue in the Northwest, as well as Tiffany & Co. And what can you find here? Some of the most popular shops in the area, including **J.Crew, Eddie Bauer, Victoria's Secret,** various **Gap** stores, **Banana Republic, Ann Taylor, Talbots, J. Jill, Louis Vuitton, BCBG, Juicy Couture,** and a **Coach** store. Once you've figured out what to wear, **Twist and Gamekeeper** will provide presents for lucky people, and **Starbucks** and **Godiva Chocolate** will supply you sustenance. **Aveda** and **Origins** also have small shops here, for a little shopping aromatherapy.

Multnomah Village

Multnomah really does feel like a village—it is a tight-knit community in addition to its identity as a retail, coffee shop, and hang-out mecca. Adding to the cohesive feel are the wonderful **Multnomah Arts Center,** 7688 Capitol Highway, a Portland arts and recreation facility offering classes in everything from acrylic painting to Zen flower arranging, and **Annie Bloom's Books,** 7834 Southwest Capitol Highway, an outstanding bookstore that draws people from all over the city. Other Village highlights include the two dozen shops of every variety. We especially like **Northwest Wools,** 3524 Southwest Troy, for beautiful yarns and other fibers; **Peggy Sunday's,** 7880 Southwest Capitol Highway, for upscale housewares; and **Birdie's Gift Shop,** 7847 Southwest Capitol Highway, for gifts, cards, and bath products.

## *Northwest Portland*

### Northwest 23rd District

This upscale, trendy neighborhood includes a number of shops on 21st, but is known to Portlanders simply as Northwest 23rd. Filled with lovely Victorian homes and countless trees, this neighborhood is one of the prettier balances of the domestic and commercial in Portland, and it's a great walking neighborhood—the pedestrian traffic here is at times so uppity that it stops the automotive traffic. The foot traffic has created a democracy of fashion: The pierced hipsters sipping martinis at the Gypsy coexist comfortably with the bourgeois denizens dining at Wildwood, and that's because there is something for everyone. Chain representatives include the **Gap,** 2303 West Burnside; **Urban Outfitters,** 2320 Northwest Westover; **Restoration Hardware,** 315 Northwest 23rd; and the **Pottery Barn,** 310 Northwest 23rd. But the local hybrids are the real draw. For cool kitchen tools and accessories for the house, stop at **Kitchen Kaboodle,** Northwest 23rd and Flanders. For the culture hound, there is **Seaplane,** 827 Northwest 23rd, which carries beautiful dresses, many of them locally designed. **Urbino**, 638 Northwest 23rd, will help you make over your house with some of the most stylish furniture and housewares around. **What's Upstairs,** 736 Northwest 23rd, carries resale, cool jeans, and locally designed jewelry. **Girlfriends,** 904 Northwest 23rd, is the Portland branch of the hip San Francisco store that sells clothing and gifts for girls and their big sisters. On the edges of the district, **Ellington Leather Goods,** which sells its sleek handbags worldwide, has an outlet store at 1533 Northwest 24th.

## Pearl District

Colonized by starving artists, then domesticated by hipsters, the Pearl District is now becoming the home of the haute bourgeoisie. Evidence of all three classes is readily apparent in the Soho of Portland. Not only are there dozens of art galleries (and a gallery walk the first Thursday night of each month) and an art school (the **Pacific Northwest College of Art,** 1241 Northwest Johnson), but the housewares, art supplies, furniture, clothing, hardware, and even light fixtures for sale in the area have a distinctly aesthetic quality to them. For clothing, try **Aubergine,** 1100 Northwest Glisan, for chic women's wear; **Michelle deCourcy,** 916 Northwest Flanders, for her signature dresses and those of designers such as Sharon Segal and Charlotte Tarantola; and **Hanna Andersson,** 327 Northwest 10th, for colorful, comfortable clothes for children and their moms. **Richard Calhoun Old Town Florist,** 404 Northwest 10th, has elegant flowers. **Hunt and Gather,** 1302 Northwest Hoyt, has beautiful custom couches. Many gift and decorating shops pervade the area: Standouts include but are by no means limited to **Versailles in the Pearl,** 904 Northwest Hoyt; **Bella Casa,** 223 Northwest 9th; and **Cielo Home and Garden,** 528 Northwest 12th.

**Oblation Papers,** 516 Northwest 12th, sells handmade cards, invitations, and

blank books. If all this walking around is making you hungry, stop at the excellent **Pearl Bakery,** 102 Northwest 9th, which supplies many restaurants in town, or **Piazza Italia,** 1129 Northwest Johnson, for a tiny bit of North Beach. **In Good Taste,** 231 Northwest 11th, can give you cooking supplies and lessons, if you'd rather go home to eat. **Patagonia,** 907 Northwest Irving, is in the Ecotrust Building, a century-old riverside warehouse undergoing a "green" renovation. Brewery Blocks north of Burnside between 11th and 12th contains a **Sur le Table** satellite and a shiny **Whole Foods** market. The Pearl covers a large amount of territory, so wear good walking shoes when you shop here. If you need to buy them, you'll be in good shape, however, since several sporting apparel stores are clustered in the western end of the Pearl: **Lucy,** 1015 Northwest Couch, sells women's (nonshoe) gear for yoga, biking, running, and other sports; **Adidas Heritage Store,** 1039 Northwest Couch, sells vintage-style and other fabulous-looking sportswear; **REI,** 1405 Northwest Johnson, carries serious sports equipment and clothing for men, women, and children who participate in actual athletic practices other than shopping; and so does **Title 9,** 1335 Northwest Kearney, only just for women.

**Powell's City of Books**
1005 West Burnside St.
(503) 228-4651
www.powells.com

Powell's is getting pretty close to an empire. (And yes, there is a Powell: Michael Powell is the mind and the will behind Powell's growth, positioning, and well-known civic involvement.) With more than a million books in a store covering several levels in a building filling an entire city block, Powell's is the largest bookstore in the country. It even has its own (small) parking garage. Powell's has become an attraction in its own right and really does deserve a visit . . . or two . . . or three. This is a maze of a store, so pick up a map as you enter.

Sections are color-coded, and there are plenty of signs to direct you. The staff is helpful, courteous, and knowledgeable in case you have to ask directions.

## Southeast Portland
### Hawthorne District

The Hawthorne District is Portland's left-coast hip shopping area, where granola meets granita. **Powell's** on Hawthorne, 3723 Southeast Hawthorne, and **Powell's Books for Cooks,** 3747 Southeast Hawthorne, are the eastside siblings of the City of Books, and these are smaller and less overwhelming but still feature a fantastic selection and major literary events. If you've brought the little ones along, a stop at the toy store **Kids at Heart,** 3445 Southeast Hawthorne, is a must; then drag them to **Presents of Mind,** 3633 Southeast Hawthorne, to pick up a bijou for yourself—it has a play area for children so you can concentrate on the jewelry, photo albums, cards, and other trinkets. Music lovers will find Hawthorne especially fruitful. **Crossroads Music,** 3130 Southeast Hawthorne, is a music seller's co-op, and the selection of recordings and equipment here is astonishing. **The CD/Game Exchange,** 1428 Southeast 36th, is a smaller venue with a great selection of used CDs. **Jackpot Records,** 3574 Southeast Hawthorne, specializes in rare, independent, and avant-garde music, and carries new and used recordings. **Artichoke Music,** 3130 Southeast Hawthorne, will help you make music instead of merely listening to it; they carry musical instruments. Need something to wear? Try **Fyberworks,** 4300 Southeast Hawthorne, for casual, stretchy women's clothing. **Imelda's,** 3426 Southeast Hawthorne, is a destination shoe store for fashionistas all over town (it also carries shoes for men); **Red Light,** 3590 Southeast Hawthorne, brings the same crowd for vintage clothes. **American Apparel,** 3412 Southeast Hawthorne, will help you achieve a modernized '70s look. Hawthorne is the earthier alternative to the slick Northwest 23rd shopping district: You're more likely to get a whiff of patchouli than Chanel No. 5, although the **Perfume House,** 3328 Southeast Hawthorne, can supply either one.

## LoBu

On the east side of the Willamette River, Lower Burnside, or "LoBu," has a number of terrific restaurants and shops. We love **Ivy Studio,** 800 East Burnside, which carries men's and women's clothing and accessories—as does **Hattie's Vintage,** 729 East Burnside. **Moshi Moshi,** 811 East Burnside, is your source for cute and weird collectible things from Japan. More stores are opening all the time here, since LoBu is the neighborhood of the moment, and after shopping you may not want to leave. If so, linger at the **Doug Fir Lounge,** 830 East Burnside, and if you want to linger even more, stay over at the incredibly hospitable **Jupiter Hotel,** 800 East Burnside; see our Accommodations chapter.

## Sellwood District

Sellwood, one of Portland's most distinctive and historic neighborhoods, is brimming with charming antiques stores, particularly in the area along Southeast 13th Avenue, which is known as Antique Row. Because the shopping area is so condensed, you can park your car and then get around on foot. Laced in between the dozen blocks of antiques and collectibles stores, you'll find numerous delightful espresso shops and cafes.

Many shopkeepers hang signs on their buildings explaining their original use and date of construction, but our sources say that Sellwood has been known as Portland's antiques source since the 1950s. Since Sellwood was once a city in its own right (annexed in 1890), pride in the neighborhood runs deep. One could easily spend a day or two checking out the many stores, and if you do, keep an eye out for the **Sellwood Antique Collective,** 8027 Southeast 13th, for eclectic variety; the **Den of Antiquity,** 1408 Southeast Knapp for general antiques acquired with a loving eye; and **R. Spencer,** 8130

Southeast 13th, for a fine collection of furniture. (And while you're on that end of town, stop by the **Columbia Sportswear Outlet,** 1323 Southeast Tacoma, for great buys on last season's jackets.) The **Grand Central Bakery,** 7987 Southeast 13th, will refresh you with delicious soups and sandwiches before you head over to the Milwaukie Avenue section of Sellwood, which is actually called Westmoreland. There you will find **Stars,** a behemoth of antiques and collectibles. They are found at 7030 Southeast Milwaukie. For things that no one else has owned before, two good bets are the **Jealous Gardener,** 7011 Southeast Milwaukie, a cute garden and gift shop, and **Haggis**

**McBaggis,** 6802 Southeast Milwaukie, for truly wonderful children's shoes and accessories. Haggis McBaggis is so family friendly that they encourage local parents to stop by and use the attractive bathroom if their kids need a diaper change. If you're not at the diaper-changing stage yet, but would like to be, **Tres Fabu,** on the corner of Milwaukie and Bybee, has fabulous wedding gowns and everything to go with them.

### Northeast Portland
Broadway District

Northeast Broadway is a lively east-west stretch of shops, cafes, and offices; its bike-and-foot-friendly design has helped to make it one of the most enjoyable shopping districts in the city. Some—by no means all—of the major shopping attractions include **Oh Baby,** 1811 Northeast Broadway, for luscious lingerie; and **Halo,** 1425 Broadway, for the most stylish shoes. **Broadway Books,** 1714 Northeast Broadway, is an active, independent bookstore that carries a fine selection of history, local writers, and children's literature. **Dava Bead and Trade,** 1815 Northeast Broadway, will supply all your beads, findings, and other materials. **Emily Jane,** 1428 Northeast Broadway, carries beautiful handmade contemporary jewelry in a range of prices. **Kitchen Kaboodle,** at 1520 Northeast Broadway, has been purveying fine kitchenware and Northwest-casual furniture for more than 25 years; the **Goodnight Room,** 1517 Northeast Broadway, will outfit your child's room; and **Mimi & Lena,** 1914 Northeast Broadway, has high-end, cutting-edge clothes for women and their well-clad offspring. The anchor of all this glittery commerce is the **Lloyd Center,** Oregon's first indoor mall.

# Index

Photos on pages 2, 8, 13, 26, 33, 47, 69, 83, 108 courtesy of Travel Portland (visit www.Travel Portland.com). Photos on pages 5, 15, 42 courtesy of Rachel Dresbeck. Photos on pages 6, 19, 22, 53, 65, 76, 78, 85, 89, 106, 121 © Shutterstock.

Written by: Rachel Dresbeck; Layout: Joanna Beyer; Design: Diana Nuhn; PopOut maps: Maps created by Design Maps Inc. © Morris Book Publishing, LLC

Library of Congress Cataloging-in-Publication Data is available on file.

ISBN 978-0-7627-5323-9

Printed in China

10 9 8 7 6 5 4 3 2 1